MINDFUL MUSIC AND DANCING

BY STEPHANIE FINNE

BLUE OWL
BOOKS

TIPS FOR CAREGIVERS

Social and emotional learning (SEL) helps children manage emotions, create and achieve goals, maintain relationships, learn how to feel empathy, and make good decisions. The SEL approach will help children establish positive habits in communication, cooperation, and decision-making. By incorporating SEL in early reading, children will be better equipped to build confidence and foster positive peer networks.

BEFORE READING

Talk to the reader about what he or she enjoys about music or dancing.

Discuss: What do you enjoy more: music or dancing? Why? How does that activity make you feel?

AFTER READING

Discuss how the reader can add music, dancing, or both to his or her mindfulness routine.

Discuss: Can you set aside time each day to listen to music or dance? How can you use music or dancing to focus on the present moment?

SEL GOAL

Some students may struggle to identify their feelings and tune into their inner sensations and emotional experiences. This makes it hard for them to control their impulses and regulate their behaviors. Help readers develop these skills by learning to tune into their minds and bodies. Music, rhythm, and dancing can help readers slow down, focus on the present, and control their breathing.

TABLE OF CONTENTS

CHAPTER 1

MUSIC AND MINDFULNESS

Mindfulness means being in the present moment. When we are mindful, we pay attention to our **emotions**. You can practice being mindful with music and dance.

Listening to music and paying attention to a song's **rhythm** can help you **focus**. It can help slow your breathing and calm your mind.

Making music and writing songs can also help you focus and **express** your emotions. Dancing helps connect your mind and body. These are all ways to be mindful!

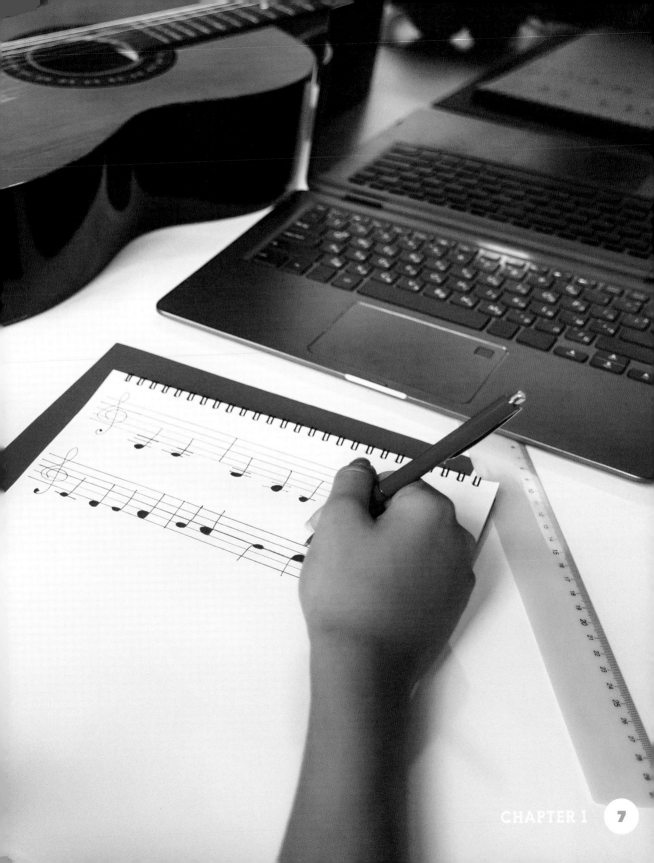

CHAPTER 2

FIND YOUR RHYTHM

Making music is about finding your own rhythm. Before you begin, set your **intention**. What types of sounds do you want to make? What emotions do you want to express?

You don't need an instrument to make music. You can use everyday objects, such as pots, pans, and spoons. Or you can listen to music and clap the beat.

Listening to music mindfully helps us focus on our breathing and feelings.

Step 1: Think about how you are feeling.

Step 2: Play a song and listen closely. Try to tune out whatever is going on around you. What sounds do you hear? If there is singing, what are the **lyrics** about?

Step 3: Pay attention to your breathing. Does it change? Does your body **react** in other ways? How do you feel after the song ends?

MUSIC GENRES

Music **genres**, such as classical and metal, are very different. They can affect your emotions in different ways. Try listening to different kinds of songs. Notice how each makes you feel.

HELPFUL HINT: Your drum can be anything that makes a sound when tapped or banged on.

Drumming can be a good way to express your emotions.

Step 1: Think about how you are feeling. Start drumming a beat that matches your emotions.

Step 2: Pay attention to the beat. Is it fast or slow? Does it match what you are feeling?

Step 3: Focus on your hands and arms. How do they feel when they tap the beat?

MUSIC FOR YOU

No matter what kind of music you make, it can be just for you. Some people like to perform, but your music can be for your eyes and ears only.

Writing lyrics about what you are feeling in a song **journal** can also help you express your emotions.

Step 1: Find a notebook you can use for songwriting. It can be for your eyes only.

Step 2: Write each day for 10 to 15 minutes. It doesn't matter what you write! Here is one idea:

- What are you feeling right now? What words would you use to describe those feelings?

Step 3: Hum or whistle a **melody** to put with your lyrics. Sing the song you wrote. Experiment and see what feels right to you!

HELPFUL HINT: Writing each day can help you form a **habit** of expressing yourself.

CHAPTER 3

DANCE TO TUNE IN

Dancing is another way to be mindful. When learning a new dance, you have to pay close attention to the steps. This helps you focus and stay in the present moment.

Dancing also helps you tune into your body. As you listen to music, notice how your body reacts. Does your foot tap to the beat? Does your heart beat faster?

Dancing can help you express yourself.

Step 1: Find a song you enjoy.

Step 2: Close your eyes and listen to the music. Move your body to the rhythm. You can tap or stomp your feet, twirl, or jump around!

Step 3: Pay attention to how your body moves. Keep dancing for as long as you want! When you are done, take a break to **reflect**. How does your body feel? Did dancing change your mood?

DANCE LIKE NO ONE IS WATCHING

Dancing may feel awkward or silly. Try not to judge if a movement is good or bad. Just have fun and focus on moving your body!

When being mindful, the **process** is the important part. Pay attention to how dancing makes you feel. Keep working on your music until it feels right.

Afterward, check in with your mind and body. What did music do for you?

GOALS AND TOOLS

GROW WITH GOALS

Making music and dancing mindfully can help keep you in the moment and tuned in. Try these things:

Goal: Focus on your breathing as you listen to a song.

Goal: Pay attention to how each muscle moves as you dance.

Goal: Read song lyrics you have written without judgment. Everything you create is special.

TRY THIS!

Freeze dancing is a fun way to be mindful while moving. Have a friend or adult help you with this activity. He or she will pause the music whenever they like.

1. Check in with how you are feeling.

2. When the music plays, dance any way that feels right to you.

3. When the music stops, FREEZE! Is your breathing fast or slow? How does your body feel?

4. Continue dancing every time the music starts. Freeze when it stops. When you are done, think about your experience. Then it's your turn to freeze the music for your friend!

GLOSSARY

emotions
Feelings, such as happiness, sadness, or anger.

express
To show what you feel or think with words, writing, or actions.

focus
To concentrate on something.

genres
Particular kinds of creative work.

habit
An activity or behavior that you do regularly, often without thinking about it.

intention
Something you mean to do.

journal
A diary in which one regularly writes down his or her experiences, thoughts, and feelings.

lyrics
The words of a song.

melody
An arrangement of musical notes that makes a tune.

mindfulness
A mentality achieved by focusing on the present moment and calmly recognizing and accepting your feelings, thoughts, and sensations.

process
A series of actions or steps that produces a particular result.

react
To behave in a particular way as a response to something that has happened.

reflect
To think carefully or seriously about something.

rhythm
A repeated pattern of sound or movement in music, dance, or poetry.

TO LEARN MORE

Finding more information is as easy as 1, 2, 3.

1. Go to www.factsurfer.com

2. Enter "**mindfulmusicanddancing**" into the search box.

3. Choose your book to see a list of websites.

INDEX

Blue Owl Books are published by Jump!, 5357 Penn Avenue South, Minneapolis, MN 55419, www.jumplibrary.com

Copyright © 2022 Jump! International copyright reserved in all countries. No part of this book may be reproduced in any form without written permission from the publisher.

Library of Congress Cataloging-in-Publication Data

Names: Finne, Stephanie, author.
Title: Mindful music and dancing / by Stephanie Finne.
Description: Minneapolis: Jump!, Inc., 2022.
Series: The art of mindfulness | Includes index. | Audience: Ages 7–10
Identifiers: LCCN 2021033542 (print)
LCCN 2021033543 (ebook)
ISBN 9781636903644 (hardcover)
ISBN 9781636903651 (paperback)
ISBN 9781636903668 (ebook)
Subjects: LCSH: Music—Instruction and study—Activity programs. | Dance—Study and teaching (Elementary)
Music and dance—Juvenile literature. | Mindfulness (Psychology)—Juvenile literature.
Classification: LCC MT948 .F457 2022 (print) | LCC MT948 (ebook) | DDC 372.87—dc23
LC record available at https://lccn.loc.gov/2021033542
LC ebook record available at https://lccn.loc.gov/2021033543

Editor: Jenna Gleisner
Designer: Michelle Sonnek

Photo Credits: LattaPictures/iStock, cover; stanley45/iStock, 1; Apollofoto/Shutterstock, 3; Donna Ellen Coleman/Shutterstock, 4; Prostock-studio/Shutterstock, 5; portishead1/iStock, 6–7; Sergey Novikov/Shutterstock, 8; Kues/Shutterstock, 9; Fertnig/iStock, 10–11; LumiNola/iStock, 12–13; PRASANNAPIX/Shutterstock, 14–15; iStock, 16; Asier Romero/Shutterstock, 17; Dean Drobot/Shutterstock, 18–19; Africa Studio/Shutterstock, 20–21.

Printed in the United States of America at Corporate Graphics in North Mankato, Minnesota.